The New Apostolic Reformation: The Church in the Locality

By Stan DeKoven

The New Apostolic Reformation:
The Church in the Locality

By Stan DeKoven

Copyright © 2016 by Stan DeKoven

ISBN 978-1-61529-179-3

Vision Publishing
1115 D Street
Ramona, CA 92065

All rights reserved worldwide.

No part of this book may be reproduced in any manner without the written permission of the author except in brief quotations embodied in critical articles of review.

Table of Contents

Foreword 5
The New Apostolic Reformation (NAR) 9
Concluding Thoughts 23
Vision International University and Vision
   International Training and Education Network 27

Foreword

For thirty years I have been a professor of church growth. One of my tasks has been to undertake the necessary research to answer the following four questions:

- Why does the blessing of God rest where it does?
- Since it is obvious that not all churches are equal, why is it that at certain times and in certain places some churches seem to be more blessed than others?
- Can any pattern of divine blessing on churches be discerned?
- If so, what are the salient characteristics of unusually blessed churches?

It has now become clear that at this particular point of history, the unusual blessing of God is resting on what I like to call churches of "The New Apostolic Reformation." This does not mean that God is not blessing some other churches as well. But it does derive from the fact that in virtually every part of the world the fastest growing group of churches are New Apostolic Churches.

Not everybody is aware that these churches even exist. Many who do realize this have discovered no way to infiltrate and understand the New Apostolic Churches. But my friend, Stan DeKoven is one who does. As the President of Vision International University, he has been deeply involved in training cutting-edge leadership for New Apostolic Churches.

Stan's fingerprints are all over these churches!

In this booklet, Dr. Stan has addressed the questions relating to the pattern of today's divine blessing, and the salient characteristics of the blessed churches. Stan accurately sees that the Church in the 21st Century will be the Church which exhibits these characteristics.

But he goes beyond that assessment.

Dr. DeKoven probes the reasons why New Apostolic Churches are such a driving force for the Kingdom, showing through careful research that they are, from their roots up, biblical churches. They adhere to the fundamental patterns established by God in the Old Testament and in the intertestamental period, and they also have been molded by the governmental pattern taught by Jesus and practiced by the apostles.

All this is to say that the book you have in your hands can be regarded as a biblical theology of the New Apostolic Reformation. It goes hand in hand with other books describing this dynamic movement from empirical, sociological or methodological perspectives. I will be recommending Stan DeKoven's book because I know it will build their confidence that the ways that they have come to understand as the Church are ways near to the heart of God.

> C. Peter Wagner, Chancellor
> Wagner Leadership Institute

*The True Church can never fail.
For it is based upon a rock.*
– T.S. Eliot

*The perfect church service would be one we were almost
unaware of. Our attention would have been on God.*
– C.S. Lewis

The New Apostolic Reformation(NAR)

Over the last several years there have been many attempts made to define what Gods intention is for the church. The church is God's instrument for the expansion of his Kingdom, yet in many ways, due to cultural changes and challenges, the church is struggling in the uncharted waters of the 21st Century. Many a Christian leader has clamored for a return to 1st Century Church Christianity, a Christianity filled with *awe* and the fear of the Lord, where the power of God was regularly manifested through the gifts of the Holy Spirit, and where hundreds and thousands of men and women came streaming into the Kingdom of God confessing their sins and turning from a lifestyle abhorrent to God and his Word.

Through the centuries we've seen many types of church government and ways of defining and developing church life for the needs of God's people and for the reaching of a lost and dying world. Some have been more successful than others. But one thing is certain; in each subsequent generation God does a new thing, not new in its essence, but different than what has ever been done before —yet new in terms of its paradigm or its way of accomplishing the purpose of God for that generation. Many key observers of church life such as Dr. C. Peter Wagner are openly describing a new paradigm emerging in the church today. This paradigm is right for this Kairos time of change in American culture. It has been coined the New Apostolic Reformation, a return to the New Testament patterns, yet contextualized to present culture.

A New Paradigm

The New Apostolic Reformation envisions a return or a restoration of many biblical concepts. These include restored offices, (the Five-fold ministry in full operation, Ephesians 4:11-16), or ascension gifts, as given by Christ to the Church, (seen as still functional today). Many believe that the role of the apostle and prophet are no longer needed now that we have the fullness of scripture. But many leaders conclude that we are in desperate need of true apostolic and prophetic ministry, which are considered foundation-building for the local church. The restored offices of the apostle and prophet work in tandem to lay proper biblical foundations. The prophet speaks the vision of God for a circumstance or situation, the apostle puts the vision into practice, working along with teachers, pastors and evangelists, together with lay leaders (the priesthood of all believers). Together they build the local church, bringing God's people to maturity in the faith. Until fairly recently, seeing the five-fold ministry functioning together was simply in the imagination of the idealist. But many leaders worldwide are beginning to lay down personal agendas, networking for the greater purposes of God as these restored offices are coming into maturity.

Local Church or Church of the Locality?

Along with a renewed emphasis on the apostolic/prophetic Ministry, there is a renewed understanding of the church of the locality versus the individual local congregation. In essence, the NAR is redefining what local church is all about. Local churches as defined in the New Testament were made up of individual congregations within a city or locality. When the Apostle Paul wrote to a church he did so to the church in Ephesus, a city, or to the churches in Galatia, a region. He did not write to the First Baptist Church or to the First Assembly of God or to the First Independent Church. He wrote to the elders within that city. Elders consist of the five-fold ministry gifts including pastors, evangelist, teachers, apostles and prophets working together in a city or region, along with ruling elders and deacons who gave oversight to local congregations. A plurality of elders existed with responsibility of ministry to the local assembly (ecclesia), whereas five-fold ministry were responsible to the larger body of Christ. Thus, in the NAR, proper government of the church is being discussed openly and necessary adjustments are being made.

Further, in this new paradigm we are seeing rebuilt foundations. Most local churches are founded by pastors, evangelists or teachers, specifically reflecting those unique giftings. However, according to the Word of God (Ephesians 2:20) it is the apostolic and prophetic ministries working together that lay the proper foundation for the growth of a church within a locality. Thus, there is a renewed interest and emphasis on apostolic and prophetic church planting, where local churches are being planted in communities everywhere. Church planting is the definition of true revival.

Along with a renewal of church planting as a primary mandate, we are seeing a restructured church government. One of the predominant ministries of the apostle is to establish ministries and bring correction to the government of the church. Working together with seasoned prophets in presbytery, they give necessary input to assist congregations and ministries to grow. These anointed leaders give relational oversight to local congregations, assisting them in their growth and development to reach their community for Christ.

Through the dynamic of teaching, the various ministries are emerging. Further, various gifts within God's people are beginning to emerge as five-fold ministry leaders and elders are recognizing the mandate for the priesthood of all believers, male and female, in every capacity, to be functional within the church of the locality.

Finally, we are beginning to see the emergence of convening counsels, where key leaders within the body of Christ gather in a region together to dialog and debate doctrinal issues to bring the wisdom of God to bear upon his church. This was a dynamic of the 1st century church (Acts 15) where the Jerusalem counsel determined that the Gentiles were not required to become circumcised Jews in order to inherit the kingdom of God. These convening or apostolic counsels/companies are developing team ministry within local communities for the purpose of planting churches and establishing ministries, both local and trans local.

In other words, what is beginning to emerge is a maturing of the body of Christ, which is recognizing the various New Testament patterns of ministry, and implementing them with a sense of urgency as we prepare for the return of our Lord Jesus Christ. (1st Timothy 2:2 and Acts 19)

A New Testament Definition of Revival

As a part of the New Apostolic Reformation there are new definitions of what revival is. Many have indicated that revival consists of various and sundry renewals of the people of God with unique manifestations the result. Without being overly critical of these manifestations, we must recognize that in the midst of much of what can be clearly criticized from various renewal movements, there has been the hand of God; manifesting his mercy and grace upon God's people. Yet we cannot, we dare not, call these manifestations revival. In fact, revival must be defined purely from a New Testament biblical model. First, it's the renewal of the understanding of the Great Commission as described in Matthew 28: 18-20 and Acts 1:8. Secondly, the result of this overwhelming passion for God was church planting; first in strictly Jewish communities, then progressively to the whosoever will worldwide. Though there are many patterns for church government in the modern church, all having some component of New Testament patterns, a true hunger has emerged amongst New Apostolic Reformation leaders to return to New Testament patterns of Christianity. To do so we must review the three primary church models found in the book of Acts... Jerusalem, Antioch, and Ephesus.

The Tale of Three Churches:
The Pattern for Church Development

In many ways the Church in Jerusalem missed the grand opportunity of taking the gospel to the Gentiles. Their mono-cultural focus limited their ability to reach beyond their comfort zone. It was predominantly through the ministries of Barnabus and Paul that multicultural ministry was established. (Acts 11, Acts 13)

The focus of ministry for the Apostle Paul, Barnabus and later Silas and others was to plant churches everywhere. Acts 14 indicates that not only did they plant churches, but these churches provided mutual support to one another in the development of the Kingdom of God.

Perhaps the best picture of God's plan for the church can be found in the book of Acts the 19th chapter. The Apostle Paul comes to a community where believers already existed. However, it was readily apparent that the foundation of their faith had been inadequately laid. Paul ensured that the believers were baptized in water, filled with the Spirit, and released into the gifts of the Holy Spirit, before proceeding further in church life: the foundation had to be rebuilt.

Then for the next two years he taught them daily, releasing them periodically into ministry to preach the gospel, cast out demons, and bring healing to those that were oppressed of the devil. This was done throughout the entire region.

So much was the influence of the Apostle Paul and his disciple's ministry that fear came upon the people; even the economic climate of the community changed. Most importantly, all of Asia Minor received the gospel of the Kingdom, and churches were planted to glorify God.

This is still the heart cry of every New Apostolic Reformation leader: to see the power of God released and the Kingdom of God expanded everywhere, through the planting of indigenous, relationally connected local congregations.

Setting the House in Order

A final component of the New Apostolic Reformation is an understanding of the qualities of a truly healthy church. The heart of an apostle in true Fatherly ministry is to see God's house set in order. Christian A. Schwartz has summarized the signs of a healthy church. His research, with authors commentary, is presented here.

1. **The empowering of leadership**. In the New Apostolic Reformation, superstars are not the norm nor are they needed. Instead, men and women who are servant leaders with the emphasis on servanthood first are required and desired. Their leadership will be strong and dynamic, but with a specific purpose of the establishment of the Kingdom of God, not their own kingdom.
2. A healthy New Apostolic Reformation Church will be **gift-oriented in its ministry** — that is, the lay ministry will be released. Platform oriented, personality driven ministry, which is highly problematic, will be minimized. The recognition of the gifts and calling of men and women will determine what will happen within congregational life.

   The Apostle Paul determined in the latter days of his life to know no man or woman by the flesh, but by the Spirit; that is, he would know them by their fruit and gifting.

The Church is beginning to grow-up, able to recognize gifts and calling, avoiding the pursuit of "the anointed ones" for pure, healthy, Christian character in action.

3. There is a **passionate spirituality** as a part of a healthy church. When I say passionate, I mean they have a pursuit for God. They want to know Him as Paul did in the power of his resurrection and in the fellowship of his sufferings, to be conformed unto his death. More than anything else they want to be intimate with the Lord Jesus Christ, filled with the purpose of God.
4. New Apostolic Reformation Churches have **functional structures** rather than rigidly formed forms of operation. Their structures will be functional, contextualized to the local community in which they live.

There are many ways to reach people for Christ; there are many tools available to us today. None of these tools are in and of themselves good or bad as long as we are preaching the gospel of Christ.

The key is to find the structures that work within a local context. Churches must be able to change rapidly, especially in the day and time that we live, and New Apostolic Reformation Churches have functional structures that are able to reach their community in unique ways.

5. New Apostolic Reformation Churches will have **inspiring worship services** that are filled with passion and are prophetic in focus. An atmosphere of prophecy was found in the Church in Corinth (I Corinthians 14), so much so that those who had sin were convicted. People in need of ministry were ministered to in the midst of the worship service.

Worship should include songs, hymns, and spiritual songs, making melody in the heart. Thus, the lifestyle of worship, taught by such men as Dr. Lamar Boschman becomes essential. No longer is it just singing led by a talented worship leader or performance by a group on a platform, but worship is focused on God and his majestic greatness.

Further, true leaders are recognizing the historic need for hymns to be sung as they present doctrinal pictures that can be readily learned by the uninformed and uninitiated. Our songs, hymns and spiritual songs in combination lift the congregation as we lift our voices to the Lord in gratitude and love for all that he has done.

6. There are holistic **small groups** being developed in most New Apostolic Reformation churches. Small group ministry provides a place where teaching can be enjoyed and meaningful fellowship can occur, where ministry to those in need and evangelism can be naturally expressed. New Apostolic Reformation churches are recognizing the important dynamic of small groups as a part of the overall vitality of church life.
7. **Need oriented evangelism**, where gifted men and women are trained to utilize their gifts to evangelize within various communities is emerging. Specialized programs are being developed through New Apostolic Reformation churches that are able to touch the needs of the community. They are not specifically designed just to meet needs. Their goal is to present the gospel of Christ and win people to Jesus.
8. **Loving relationships** are again the focus of church life: We must all learn to love God with our heart, soul, mind and strength, and our neighbor as ourselves. There is a new recognition of who our neighbor is.

   Our neighbor is male and female. Our neighbor is poor and rich. Our neighbor is national and international. Our neighbor is multi-cultural. All mankind needs to know the love of God. Loving relationships are becoming highly valued and emphasized within New Apostolic Reformation churches.

9. **Biblical preaching and teaching** has returned to the forefront of ministry. All five-fold ministry leaders are required to be teachers to equip God's people. Much preaching has been thematic, primarily focused on various doctrines which come from certain spiritual DNA of various spiritual "tribes".

   There is renewed recognition that we need the whole of God's word. Preaching must come from the Old Testament and the New. Further, gift ministries in NAR churches are making room for trans-local ministries who have the ability to impart life into a congregation. The goal is to make disciples, often done through church based schools of ministry rather than regional colleges and seminaries.

10. **Visionary leadership** is a key component of the New Apostolic Reformation. That is, leaders are recognizing that without a vision, the people are unrestrained. It is required of leaders to provide a vision that will motivate people in a godly direction and encourage

them to fulfill the purpose for which they have been called into community.

The Body of Christ needs charismatic people as visionary leaders with a vision that flows from the heart of God. The vision is often expressed through prophetic ministry, which is necessary for the building of a healthy church in our New Apostolic Times.

Concluding Thoughts

There have been many attempts to unify the church. However, unity for the sake of unity has little meaning. One highly encouraging sign in the church is the emergence of leaders finding each other for prayer and networking together for ministry in a city.

I have the privilege of working with such a network (City Church Ministries, founded and directed by Apostle George Runyan). The result is an increase in the church in our region. When leaders lay down their personal agendas for the greater good, Jesus' prayer in John 17 comes close to fulfillment.

Jesus prayed for unity, but the prayer that he prayed was for unity that would fulfill the purposes of the Father. Unity, especially within the city where God has placed his leaders, can produce great results. When men and women are willing to be vulnerable with each other, to support each other, pray for each other, and care for each other, regardless of the differing flavors/tribes, the purposes of God are soon to follow.

When leaders demonstrate a willingness to give to other congregations to strengthen them from their resources, whether it be with worship teams, financially, or people to assist in various areas of ministry, revival will soon follow.

Churches are beginning to network, recognizing that you will find McDonald restaurants, Burger King and Taco Bell building their stores near each other, knowing that the hungry want variety; and that we'll all benefit if we network together. So it is with churches, there's a common profit that is gained when we share with each other the resources that God has given.

Finally, good stewardship is being practiced. New Apostolic Reformation Churches have recognized that prosperity is for the purpose of establishing God's covenant. As with Abraham, we are blessed to be a blessing. God has blessed us, strengthened us and given us resources, but they're not for our own benefit. They're truly for the benefit of the greater body of Christ.

The time of change is upon us. The choices that God's chosen leaders make may well shape the church of the future. If what we are observing is true, (there is no question that our observations and comments are at present idealistic). If God is really breathing by the Holy Spirit new life into the church, bringing a paradigmatic shift from self-absorbed to other oriented, from selfish ambitious worship to God-focused adoration, from being inward in viewpoint to evangelistic church plant driven; then the Church is being prepared to transition into its greatest season in history.

The New Apostolic Reformation is upon us. May God

help us to enter his greater purposes with wisdom and knowledge that with God, all things are possible.

Vision International University and Vision International Training and Education Network

An adult education outreach in your local church!

VISION INTERNATIONAL is an educational ministry designed to assist in the task of "equipping the saints for the work of the ministry," (Ephesians 4:12). In essence, we are here to equip the equipper (provide to the local church leadership) to equip the saints of God. Our International Network of Bible Colleges in local churches spans the globe, working with pastors to develop quality-training centers for their congregation. VISION, established in 1974, has over 4,000 campuses in 150 nations, serving 100,000+ students worldwide.

In this package (and in the brief description below) you will find information regarding the services offered at VISION. Our delivery systems remain uncomplicated, with minimal administrative work for the local church. We take the hassle out of your education program. After reviewing the material, feel free to contact us. We are a service ministry with a heart for God's Kingdom, and we would be honored to further discuss the personal needs of your ministry and vision.

Who We are and What We do

Biblical Philosophy for Training

Our model for ministry training is a composite of the model exemplified by the churches at Antioch and Ephesus, both of which were founded with apostolic/prophetic ministries, apostolic in both structure and function. Within these local churches, fivefold ministers employed their special anointing and giftings in order to "equip the saints for the work of the ministry, to the building up of the Body of Christ." Then, those members of the body who had been, trained, educated under the tutelage and mentorship of the ministerial presbytery were sent forth into various forms, fields, and spheres of spiritual service and outreach.

From the beginning of the New Testament era, the Lord has used the local church and its fivefold eldership to teach and train its people for God's service. VISION partners with the local church in the fulfillment of that traditional and Scriptural calling by providing an educational tool through which the "equippers" are equipped for the work of the ministry and the laborers are prepared and sent forth for the harvest.

Our Primary Purpose and Role

- Vision International was started in 1974 due to the desperate need to train men and women for effective service. Beginning as Vision Bible College under Dr. Ken Chant in Australia and Logos Bible Institute under Drs. Joseph Bohac and Stan DeKoven in San Diego, California, it has now grown to include degree granting through the State of California and Australia, with increasing recognition around the world.

- Vision International offers local churches a "turn-key" operation for the establishment of a complete, high-quality, accredited in-house Bible College operated under its own leadership. We provide the local church a comprehensive four-year curriculum consisting of more than one hundred courses to train men and women for effective service under pastoral authority and professional mentorship.
- Vision International University and the Vision International Education and Training Network Affiliate Center Program makes it possible for Christian leaders and workers to fulfill their aspirations of completing their education and/or receiving educational credit for their experience and the expertise they have accumulated over the years of ministry service-and, all without leaving their community, family, job or local church! In fact, they can accomplish it all right at their local church under the tutelage and mentoring of local church leaders who know

them and have a keen pastoral interest in their spiritual development!

No longer does the local church need to send its young people and developing leaders off to some faraway religious academic institution with curricula far-removed from practical ministry in order to prepare them for Christian service.

- Our overall role is to assist the local church in preparing leaders for God's great end-time harvest. There is a fresh wind of God's Spirit blowing on our world today! However, our "world" requires innovative ministries with innovative delivery systems to bring the Gospel to "every nation and every tribe." Indeed, our primary focus is the same as the mandate that is upon the Church at large- "teach all nations" and "make disciples."

A College Campus at Your Local Church!

Here are some of the benefits of having a fully authorized college program in your community and under your church name:

- A powerful tool for training and equipping teachers, leaders, elders, deacons and 5-fold ministers.

- Creates excitement in the congregation with earned certificates and diplomas.
- Provides a non-traditional opportunity for people to earn a college degree.
- Designed to be financially beneficial for the local church. Most finances remain in the local community
- Promotes church growth through specially crafted courses in church ministry
- It is an excellent tool for the fulfillment of the Great Commission- to "make disciples (lit., learners) …teaching them to observe whatsoever things (Jesus) commanded (us)".
- It produces added legitimacy and credibility to the local church's ministry.
- It enhances the local church's status in the community, and is an excellent tool for reaching out beyond the walls to the local community and other churches.
- It can be an integral part of the local church's education program
- It aids in the development of in-house intermediate leadership, equipping, educating, and mentoring under the supervision of senior leadership

- It allows the local leadership greater involvement in the spiritual education of its members, developing leaders through dynamic curriculum.
- It affords in-house teachers, other fivefold ministers, and those in the various helps ministries an opportunity and structure in which to employ their gifts and talents

An Extension Campus of Vision International Retains the Harvest in your Community

Vision International

- We will extend our credentials as a fully authorized College to the local church.
- We will provide a complete program for students up to a Bachelor's Degree, with accredited courses leading to a nationally accredited degree. [1]
- We will provide a comprehensive administrative system and personnel to assist you in developing your own local education ministry
- We provide Academic Consultation for the development and maintenance of your school

---

[1] Accredited courses through the Global Christian College Credit Consortium (GC4)

- We provide all textbooks, examinations, course outlines, syllabi, catalogs, videos, etc., for your Bible College
- We are a complete Bible education ministry
- We assist you in the promotion of your college program. Transcripts and records management are handled jointly by the local campus and the International Headquarters
- We provide education opportunities for local church leaders. Academic recognition of life experience can be applied towards college completion.
- We will provide a national and international pool of instructors for annual Leadership Conferences to strengthen your local church, build leadership and promote your school
- We have adjunct staff available to teach seminars that will strengthen your ministry
- We offer a dynamic World Missions program at Vision/VITEN

Vision International is called to:

- Strengthen the local church and pastoral leadership
- Assist you in training and discipling your own people

- Help you avoid losing your potential future leadership, which often occurs when young people are sent to some distant location for training.

For more information, contact
Vision International
1115 D Street
Ramona, CA 92065
1-800 9VISION (984-7466)
www.vision.edu

Other Key Books by Dr. DeKoven

Supernatural Architecture
Journey to Wholeness
New Beginnings
Christian Education
40 Days to the Promise
On Belay!
Visionary Leadership
Leadership in the Church
Strategic Church Administration
Financial Integrity

www.booksbyvision.com

www.ingramcontent.com/pod-product-compliance
Lightning Source LLC
Chambersburg PA
CBHW061314040426
42444CB00010B/2630